45

Thought Crimes

new writing by
Lynn Breedlove

Manic D Press
San Francisco

in memoriam

Wickie Stamps
who taught me how to make crazy helpful
&
ADM
the coolest squat there ever was

45 *Thought Crimes* © 2019 Lynn Breedlove. Published by Manic D Press. All rights reserved. ISBN 978-1-945665-17-2. For information, contact Manic D Press, Box 410804, San Francisco CA 94141.   www.manicdpress.com

Author photo: Emily Jane   Printed in Canada

for
Steph Joy
co-conspirator in acts of sedition
both private and grand
who taught me a switchblade's as fine as a chainsaw

CONTENTS

I. A Call to Arms

II. A Call to Arms

I.
A Call to Arms

In Camps Even Atheists Pray

All That Is, please guide us out of this darkness. In this moment crying. In this moment sure. Laughing, fucking, eating, replicating plates served by mothers. Channeling Taurus full moon and dead moms and live dads, grounded forward going, get outta jail free, avoid jail entirely, make it happen magic, and glamour money fashion shine charm build-it action. True love always.

Bring Mandelas, Mumias, Panthers and Kings, bring Peltiers and Black Elks and Lame Deers. Bring Maya Angelou all aglow and how she says bring your ancestors with you into the room, and what will be read is power. Charisma.

All the angels, all the stars, all the ghosts of Sophie Scholl, the White Rose, von Stauffenberg, Anne Frank, and Marlene. All the nameless who gave a crust of bread to someone who wasn't gonna live anyway. All the retro planets saying save your energy till late in the game and then slingshot it through the eye of despots, blow everything sky high at once, take out killers with our high powered books and Subcultural Standards of Beauty good looks. And if you're lucky just keep reloading, picking off evil. Keep them in your sights, crosshairs the only cross you pray to or bear.

Leave behind a trail of stars to X marks the spot, to treasure, to hearts, to explosions of light, to true love coming in your fist, to high as a kite in your arms, to crying over the loss of all humans, all the queers and trans, women and children, beasts and sky and water, last but not least, all the blue sky from the west down to the east. Blue, just how we see it from here. Blow it all up, and it's a dream remembered by sentries at castles who look out at black starry skies and tell stories of what we learned there, then, on a green and blue rock, far away and once upon a time.

Typewriter

Now is the time for all good men to come to the aid of their country,
my mother would type when testing a new typewriter.

"Why do you write that?"
"Because it has almost all the letters," she'd say.

Or because she was always in a state of war,
having grown up in a holocaust.

I grew up believing that sentence was always true.
Now is no time to gaze at your navel, your dick,

or whatever shit list you make fresh everyday
to the exclusion of what is happening around you.

Integrate. Cry. Empathize.
But stand the fuck up.

Make music. Make art.
Forgive whoever is in the way.

Let go of bullshit. Acknowledge
you fucked up. Change.

Prioritize the real work, or you'll have nothing but time
to do the meaningless shit you been putting first.

1939, Chemnitz, Germany

one day, my grandfather who had a cannery and a new American car every year, whose parents had a deli, who promised his wife's parents to take care of her, who was a businessman, who had a young wife and a daughter, who did not have anything else to give, said,

"i could sign a government contract for rations for the army. make so much more money. it would be a good business deal. but i'd have to join the nazi party."

my grandmother yelled. threw things. it got heated. "over my dead body. you'll get none of this. make that money for yourself cuz i'm taking the child and leaving. don't even think about it. are you out of your old addled mind?"

my mom was pretty sure her parents were about to split up. but they didn't. he did what she said. she set him straight. she never let him sell out. she reminded him of what is right and good and true and what selling out means and who you're selling out to and that the world is so much more than this little family.

their blood runs in my veins. the man who wants to do right, sometimes unclear, who finds the rock, and she shows him what's right. the woman who sees truth and throws mandatory pictures of despots out the window and into the street, consequences be damned.

let our fierceness guide each other. let us stand up to our beloveds. let us stand for strangers. let us be strong when it's not popular. let us make our grandchildren proud.

let us change the DNA of our descendants.

Prepare for Peace

if every day you meditated on throwing babies at ships to watch
    them drop into the sea.
if you squinted into Ford headlights and stared down Glock
    barrels,
if you were guillotined for flipping leaflets into an atrium
if you risked your neck to assassinate one who's had your
    allegiance or flung photos of despots out French doors;
if you snuck a friend out with forged papers or wore a patch that
    made everyone a target instead of singling out a few,
if you taught your daughter to shoot or threw your father's Luger
    in the river,
there'd be grit enough for another lump of clay.

Stolen Histories

i. Bert

great-grandfather Bert was born on a rez near Missoula. parents looked white but he didn't. said he was a half-breed. like, whatcha gonna do with that?

when who you are is illegal and still you pipe up. when you're gay but you come out as bisexual, cuz it's easier for them. when you got nothing to do with your parents but you find your place anyway.

wore all the uniforms he could, if it meant a band, kitchen work, a play about war. pretend. put on race like chef's whites.

Dad and Grandpa didn't like Bert. a bullshitter. pompous fool. a jerk. they needed him to be real. but his realness was snatched so he embraced crazy, shouting to the sky.

Dad as a small boy proudly explained what he'd read in a science book about relative density. Bert argued, nothing is denser than water, everyone knows that.

Dad thought, this is a know-it-all who can't see a fact staring him in the face. spot it ya got it. argue any point. it focuses the mind. a Breedlove trait, like the bump on the backs of our ears.

Bert knew things white men didn't. it'll drive you crazy to stay one foot in your world, one in the cement into which your descendants sink soul-heartedly.

you throw codes their way, maps of mountains, hunting, water, a way back, that flutter to the ground like flyers off a balustrade.

to stay true, he married a woman from Acadia, where the French escaping persecution in ships, landed and married up. the Mi'kmaq allowed it. the French were poets.

Bert passed to us a vague, intuitive dedication to Indian-ness. when truth is removed, fill in the blanks. shoot blanks. when they ask you if you're Indian, look blank. Mel Blanc. crack jokes. distract. when you see a cracked mirror, look away.

ii. Lourdes

my grandfather who tried to look away from his Indian-ness, married my grandmother, who didn't know she was Indian. or she looked away.

but she was drawn to this Indian with the hook nose, which might have been a French nose, or a Nez Perce or Blackfoot nose, it might have been that of a Mercure or a "sauvage." but it was strong.

my grandmother was the lovechild of The Church and an irresistible brown girl in a white dress at an Indian school. love had nothing to do with it.

she had the eyes of the Spanish priest. he had his eye on a girl. he had his mind on all the position and power and money and wine a priest could gather to himself if he were enterprising. he could have everything but women and children. but what do you give the man who has everything?

she thought, well, if i give him what he wants, it will go easier for me. a standard plan that sometimes works.

he might have been in love. he took the child gently from the arms of the young mother and carried her to an orphanage far away, where she lived in ribbons and petticoats among poor children less adorned.

the priest delighted her throughout her life with stories of a French mother who died in childbirth and her dad, a Spanish merchant marine who died at sea. sure. a guy who sails ships for money is almost like one who fucks over Indians for money. like horseshoes.

Grandma got treated right at the group home. they named her after a French saint. the priest said call me Padre, gave Lourdes a trust fund and set her up with a white woman to adopt her proper, proto-Nurse Jackie, opium junkie business lady who'd spend it all on a public indoor swimming pool.

Lourdes climbed up in the rafters overlooking all the boys in their stripy one pieces and smoked cigarettes with her cool friend Wiletha. they were a couple of lookers. they recited Shakespeare at the talent show.

Lourdes was racy. talk of the town, shooting roots upward like a banyan. she could read a mean soliloquy. mesmerize you with her danger ways. Perry, love of her life, came down with TB. she shed a tear and said:

i need a man who can pay my rent. mind if i marry your bestie? sure, he said and died, sealing him in her heart forever. so she married Buster. Bus, for short, cuz if you gave him any trouble he'd bust you in the mouth. real name Clemeth. hated that name. sounded gay. boy named Sue, sweet as rhubarb pie to Lourdes.

she was the only one who could tame him, and he was the only one who could rein her in, and the church, which was good for one thing:

she taught me how to remember right from left. you cross yourself with your right.

iii. Padre

the priest had decided to restore The Missions. famous men get favors and keep secrets. he was a Catholic celebrity. scandalously performed the Hoovers' wedding ceremony. the Hoovers were Protestant, as presidents needed to be and therefore could never be married by a Catholic but their Protestant minister called in sick on their wedding day in Carmel, and Padre was just the guy, a personal friend, who rewrote Indian history and lifted up the memory of men who committed genocide and slavery and threw Indian children in Christian schools and called them Indian schools, to teach a person to forget their language.

he took the Indian girl because he could. rules did not apply. that was also one of my great-grandfathers. besides great-grandfather Bert. i'm the offspring of rapists and half-breeds.

Indian is in my DNA. entitlement is in my DNA. lies are in my DNA. rape is in my DNA.

everyone knew their Indian-ness. which could get invalidated by science. or validated by grandma's premature white streak, which is indian. or that intense stare that she and the priest and Dad and i share, which is rapist, but also hustler, high-flyer, hotshot, self-starter.

it could all be acknowledged. integrated. honored. hated.
you could know about dirty corners, or red heritage, whitewashed.
you could imagine the illusion of separation.
you could be made of evil and beauty.

12 *Steps to the Deadbirdfest Pendulum Swing*

1. you have been invited to join a survivalist group.

2. by the family member with bumper stickers about an Idaho militia, Hillary for prison, and Obama with a Hitler mustache.

3. 90% of your family voted for Fuckhead.

4. half of them are POC and will hopefully come around in time.

5. although he voted for Hill, your dad didn't really get your tears when 45 was "elected."

6. your stepmom and he take you aside and say, "then we read more. we're sorry."

7. you're the only queer in the fam.

8. everyone allows you to play board games with their kids without snatching them away as if you were gonna eat them, and that makes you feel thankful.

9. you write down a night of apocalyptic nightmares, hug your dad and say, "i love you."

10. he says, in that understated Squint Eastwood way, "i'm glad you're my kid."

11. you kinda wanted to join the survivalist group.

12. but you wonder if, after you drove all the way to Coeur d'Alene, they just might not be that into you.

Apocalypse and Intimacy

you will make unpopular choices.
your family will abandon you.
you will, desperate, stab in the dark. miss your mark.
you will be tempted to give them what they want,
    then see you have no choice.
you will be accused of fucking over.
you will be seen as what you're not.

what matters is the heart, not the brain, not the five thousand,
    not the eight billion other hearts.

what matters is to not drift apart or hide under beds
    where monsters lurk.

stand up on it and jump in unicorn slippers,
    swinging pink and blue trans flag bats.

attend friends who switch off destructo-mode.
    mourn those who don't approve.

stick with who loves you, because of, not in spite of,
    what you choose.

tell tales of whoa.

document love proclamations in chalk on broken benches before
    rains wash them away.

say, THIS IS HARD and I AM HERE.

kung fu, wing chun, boxing, pit bull, gun range love.

impersonate Willie Mays dropping his bat behind him as he looks out at the future he's creating. say, bye-bye, baby! like when he hit a home run over the fence at Candlestick Park and jogs around the bases grinning that i-just-did-that grin.

not like when discounters sell ivanka's shit.

offer your bed, your quiet place as recuperation for a trans friend, who says I DON'T NEED THIS PART ANYMORE but i do need understanding and silence, not just adding sound waves to an already swimmy situation, but actually make swimming possible again. because i haven't been able to swim since 1992 when i suddenly saw my body but hadn't yet changed it.

bring back the 3-row stud belt. reclaim gospel, klezmer, Lakota prayer songs if they were ever yours, defy who locked you out.

say, so? i never wanted that anyway.
then come back and say, i changed my mind. hold up
I DO WANT IT, AND YOU CAN'T STOP ME.

one day you'll be asked to do something harder than you have ever done, and you can fall into the bottom of a glass, smoke yourself into oblivion, point fingers at who fucked it up royally, betrayed us all.

or you can stand for what, in a last moment, you will not regret.

Protesting Muslim Bans at Airports

call me a snowflake. cuter than a hatin dirty rotten scoundrel.

i was yelling along with everyone at the airport. it was emotional in this loud diverse crowd. i was tearing up and i looked over and i saw this guy who also couldn't yell cuz he was tearing up too.

so i went over and said, "i know, right?" or something. he couldn't speak, but later he touched my arm as he passed. "thanks."

i passed the place where i would always pick up my mom when she'd come home from europe, through customs, an old blonde white lady, of course whooshed right through.

she hadn't always been so privileged. when she got here she was a kraut, married to my dad, but still, in '56 she was assumed by most americans to have been a nazi.

i felt her spirit here today, approving, like when young germans pulled cobblestones out of the ground in east berlin and threw them at russian tanks in 1953. it didn't go as well as today's action.

in the past when i called certain right wingers fascist, mom would correct me: "don't say that. that is not fascism. you have no idea."

but now i think she would be like, "ok, THIS is fascism. be brave."

The Mother of All

we act like our moms loved us. they named us after heroes, built their hope into us, called us artists. we tried to live up to it, but glitter dulled over the years, and the smile that charmed became an imposter, tattered lace across dusty panes revealed shut-ins crouched below the sill peeking out blinds on the lookout for The Dealer.

with the mother goes murderously jealous unconditional amniotic cocktails and her bartender ways, slipping you mickeys and vision into the drink of your enemy. how can you be forgivable, knocking over everything at cash registers, her long dead voice telling you straighten up China Shop Bull? don't be a klutz.

god is a verb. no separation. tap into the universal oviduct.

Standing Rock

don't want to take up space, tell the complexities of heritage. not raised on a rez. bow out, stay out of the way, humble. keep secrets.

egomaniac filtering the world's troubles through your own. keep shit tucked away. trust someone, tell them something real once a week if they promise not to tell.

tell 52 different people a year. or you could just tell a girl. and certain indian brothers and sisters who invite you to smoke or sweat, who say you are real and needed.

don't waste time cowering. quit selling out to be a scout. but what if someone thinks you're doing service for street cred or you're a creep or just writing to process or you're a liar? hate that.

indian? you don't even know all your tribes. details covered up by racism in the form of indian schools (stealing), adoption (stealing), reservations (stealing), catholics giving you their names (stealing). shame (murder).

you don't even know your great-grandmother's name. her tribe. her ways. is that her, that light on your shoulder shining? or your great-grandfather bert?

name all the ancestors who fought or gave up or watched as their children were thrown on fires, who watched atrocities, who prayed as stank white men did things in the name of god.

dead man on a stick. why is that joke not abhorrent to you? seems good, that's why. seems fine. maybe you're just a poser, crying pretendian tears. or maybe you don't need a government paper. maybe you're embraced.

you could just own it. boycott lies. keep prayer private. maybe you're no less than or greater than.

you could do what's asked. you could honor grandmothers and grandfathers, pray to souls flying around who lived their lives to bring this end of this family tree, to this branch with no fruit, to your trans body, who only has words, who has no progeny, whose progeny is more than the two or three you coulda popped out if you had sold out.

you could carry justice to the last knockout punch.
you could set things right.

sing out. listen. let a girl love you, let a fighter show you how to stick em in the ribs.

tell truth a little at a time.
do what's asked. you could.

Upon Awakening to the Sound of Chainsaws

morning prayers deep. spurred by chainsaws cutting through
sleep. thank trees. choppers of trees. buffalo. cowboys.
cars that carry them. pipe layers. grandmothers and grandfathers.

women. perps, predators, killers of rapists.
forgiveness of killers. Indians. Catholics.
all our history.

dark. light. electrons.
protons. angels. monsters.
bad we done.

songs shared with us who forgot. voices wavering.
admission of wrongs prostrate on floors. light behind doors.
chainsaws making sentinels sawdust.

bulldozers, mace in the hands of mercenaries.
stand up. beat drums. sing down barrels of guns.
girl who changed everything under stars.

dark
where you do what you'd never in light.
salt.

War Time

power poets, who stood against racists for decades,
Meliza and Marcus got married. it's that time.
cataclysm. art saves.
birds still sing hotter than a pepper sprout.

risks small, love insurmountable.
when tsunamis hit, get your board,
or die flailing away from a buick
sailing upside down.

when She appears, pledge loyalty.
hawks perch over capp street.
the dead throw altars across the room.
you are anointed.

run their rage who fought and prayed so strong,
they had to be slaughtered, still here,
using you for next maneuvers.
take nothing lightly. honor ancients.

the brittle will be eaten. the flippant smacked.
harness apocalyptic mustang teams.
crowned, the mantle is on you.
summoned. brick off the hose, said Waits.

they burned synagogues, enslaved us
to build missions on sacred sites.
trail of tears. ghettos. killed Protestants,
like rabbis, like Tibetan monks.

un-killable, every dead soldier sows an army.
ride in naked. dive into each other's arms

at the sound of bugles, fly onto the backs
of palominos blending into golden hills.

conspiracy: secret agreement by people to commit to something wrong or illegal.

theory: coherent group of tested general propositions, commonly regarded as correct, that can be used as principles of explanation and prediction for a class of phenomena.

blame Head Fuck In Charge. helping false flag incidents along's a time honored tradition. see Reichstag Fire. blame a commie for world war 3. how easy would it be to exacerbate disaster n bring down cali before it secedes?

if we survive we'll write sci-fi because that could never be but it's easy just send a henchman to the hills of Ventura one night blame student fireworks when the lights go out, nothing to set off but M80s. a spark in the dark desert.

we watched army corps of engineers blow up dikes in the hoods of NOLA and flood everything, evacuate denizens to Texas in bare feet. don't come back! because land grabbers care about your health suddenly. while you're gone, they step in and voila! possession's 9/10 of the law. folks stuck in bumfuck, no ticket home, no say in the matter. no buck for a lawyer. ah the old south's at it again.

wait for a hurricane to hit. poser prez shoots paper towels to the people. playground of the rich, with no Puerto Ricans to fuck up Puerto Rico, it's like spring break in Haiti, El Salvador, Africa, Wall Street turns pristine beaches into shitholes and back again. You oughta thank em.

Tenderloin's got next. send the homeless to the burbs anywhere but here. make streets into retail heaven for peds, like Denmark. once walked by dealers and rollie bag ladies posing as tourists. some of us can't afford to stand out. the desperate are easy to move.

bring back good old A. Jackson. the president has declared himself a stable genius! Ministry of Truth! bring it all back. make America same as it ever was again. slavery to prison. internment to Gitmo.

Hollywood knows when they been had, down go *SNL* grads while right wingers troll malls for tweens. deny deny deny. the left will cry rehab! like they're gonna change.

the road to tarnished ideals is paved with broken treaties and the nutty and smutty. if you're right, you ain't stepping down, no. christians would rather vote for a molester than a leftie. they're in the minority but with a little intimidation at the polls... leave your white hood at home. by any means necessary. step on that. dilute it. sell an escape route.

you weaponize conscience, we'll spew scripture back at Jesus jumpers eating crab legs in naugahyde belts and cotton tighty whities. mixing fibers like that? you're going to hell. nam didn't end well, hearts and minds not for sale after all. nothing but a boss to lose.

then came Anita but we gave her pie on youtube. nothing sweeter than meringue on a loop. you were already brewing bugs to kill queers, trans, poor peeps, black folks, poor. black. trans. triple 7s. you missed us, don't try to kiss us. like Compton's ladies, we let sugar shakers fly. hornets nest upset. you shoulda left that baseball bat.

may the crows sleep in so songbirds sing sweetly through my window. let them herald in the morning.

may the bees hum among the jasmine budding in the pale blue dawn and the tulip tree that never stops. the bees have mostly died in a bee genocide, and wasps are left to pollinate, and flies, but they make no hives. land of milk and honey, what's become of us. we stress and look to glow boxes in our hands for calm, but no response. mouthguard sales are up.

please, bees, come home. don't let cellphones drive you away, push you out. we're sorry. we don't need them. come back. stay with your fuzzy selves, with your golden fur coats and matching slippers. come home to us.

the trees stay in bloom all year long to beckon and beg. the girl i love buys roses at the market, and they live for weeks in hopes of a suitor in a gold suit, but no one comes. virgin blooms become old maids and drop their petals, listing, unvisited.

please bees, come home. come back. we're sorry. we don't need a potion sprayed out the ass end of planes, dusting endless almond groves, don't need a patent on god's good seeds. it's you. you're all we need. come home, bees.

Old Soldiers

we train, build hard astral bodies. private stories tossed into public rings.

unskilled sons of heroes, heritage to inspire, honor who came before, remember we sabotaged gifts, calluses where scabs became scars, nerves mercifully dead, crawl over glass and under barbed wire and live rounds, brush up on old skills for wars we thought would never come.

push-ups for her, the favorite drill sergeant, secret crush in a Smokey the Bear hat, who gives you the juice to run in hard hats and backpacks without gut straps on cold mornings and hot days.

you signed up because of hot girls in dress greens, stripy suits, offering visions of kidney-shaped swimming pools, suddenly swapped for the red clay of Georgia boot camp, where little James Brown got his education in streets and whorehouses and moonshine bars, too late to back out, indoctrinations begin, the growing up, smoke em if you got em and then run, because you're young, clean your rifle of red sand and don't call it a gun.

all to help you one day against the despot you'd never foresee, to become the patriot you never thought you'd be.

first sergeant called you out of KP to say ARE YOU A HOMO-SEXUAL? you denied, laughed in your sleeve, arms behind you, parade rest.

how could you know you'd need skills like this? your mama always told you it could happen anywhere.

and now all the dead heroes you couldn't drag off fields, old officers who escaped fracking before fracking meant earth-fucking, when it meant kill your leaders cuz they led you to ambush, old butches with buzz cuts now legal cannon fodder, boys giving BJs in barracks that got them booted, and Kristin Beck all now in danger of once more not allowed to die for their country with honor, who just want a flag on their casket, dammit, all the girls swooped, frozen in a swing-dance backbend by sailors and military men in Manhattan, consent waived, for them you revive rusty skills, salute the rainbow and sing, "gave proof through the night that our fags were still there."

for them, replace fife and drums with amp and toms, slinging in a rubber band on the hood of a truck. sign up to take shots like a bike messenger dodging raindrops.

futile. but you ain't made o' sugar.

Harvey's Kids

in the middle of a square — where i once hiked in boots loaded with Stoli, pockets stuffed with baggies of head gear, re-arrangers, clouds, sharpeners, distractors, killers of pain and brain cells, of love, tears, of anything but the upper crust of a heart, veneer over bruises from life's uppercuts that had no time to heal before layering on more gold leaf — in that square, we erect chickenwire.

cut flowers, set candles, love altar to the man i at once revered and ignored as a child, even as he gave me balls to be, and playtime to revel in streets half-naked before men in blue, to kiss girls older than me on places i was made to learn, bring six-foot-tall queens with cellophane bobs to suburban schools in hot pants, ride busses to malls with trans ladies, fall in love with mean women, shoot lavender, crash scooters in rain laughing "it's our gayborhood though we're all dying," as ghosts flying around my head carried me, kept me floating above slick asphalt, showering me with heart-shaped confetti.

in that square, a man asks for water and gets not a sponge full of vinegar but a half-drunk plastic bottle with my cooties on it.

i'm the young man in this picture, not because i'm so much younger than the prophet's apprentice, but because when Harvey died, i was drowning my own sorrows over having been traded to another team, so besotted, whiskey soaked, cocaine addled, i could pay no attention to the turning of the world, no matter how relevant its rhythms.

i hand over the water, not knowing, to a living legend, not knowing it's anyone but a guy who says he has to speak and needs water, a request i have often made across a bar, begging charity from strangers.

the guy extends his hand and says, "I'm Cleve." and so, with the
water, the hero's given a secret tickertape parade before he takes
the mic and promises,

it's not over when you find your mentor assassinated, or when
you want to kill yourself at 15, or when all your friends die, or
when this asshole hijacks the election.

it's the beginning, like every cataclysm, if one lives to be blessed
with time, death, words, crowds, capacity to lament, an explosion,
a one-inch punch, the impossible seven hundred pounds of
pressure to the chest that only the occasional Bruce Lee can
deliver, but with study, anyone dedicated at Shao Lin can learn,
can stop or start a heart, break the ribs that so tentatively hold the
beating muscle that inspires young girls to ink anatomical winged
hearts to mark the spot where everything changes,

now, and now, and now.

Catalyst

the next right thing — as i told the young gay in my backseat on his way to plan a sex party, where "everyone will get so obliterated on ecstasy and ketamine, they won't even know what they want at 3 a.m., and that's when the party REALLY starts" — is start a band, fall in love, hit the streets.

that's where the action is.

there will always be those drawn to oblivion as jackboots approach. there's a measure of autonomy in hastening the end, to change the rate but not the result, as in chemistry, the causing or accelerating of a chemical change by the addition of a catalyst.

some will soldier, command, or obey. do all this, and make something beautiful or ugly out of life, but make something, for as you do, it makes you.

Sam Clam's Disco, Back in the Day

downhill from boystown, bar fulla players drinking like there's no tomorrow cuz there isn't, and softball's like pool. you can smoke and never lose. it's just about yelling and scratching and booze and your babe of the day in the bleachers, and you look good in stripy socks.

down the way is a store fulla books about wimmin, no men, and you can pick up a girl in the aisle and never worry she'll ask you to walk down one. that woody killer hasn't even been dreamed up yet. you're safe to profess your love all day.

the other way is a dark and gloomy bathhouse, haunted house ride. why don't you feel right there? you should but you don't and don't know why. you come from the easy bay and it seems dirty. naked seems like nope, but you don't know how to say no, or that they're saying no to your pals, trans sisters with whom you wanna trade stuff and treasure chests. here, have mine.

you both wish you could and that everyone wouldn't think so much about junk, but here it is right out in front. they tell you relax, but you can't. undercurrents of cis below floating tits makes them free like a skinhead rally dressed up like a picnic, bait and switch.

this town got fast turnaround, still it's whack-a-mole, growing pain communiques, like cleaning your room every day.

and down the road Esta Noche's Latinx sisters let you visit them at home, making shows of their lives like Finocchio's, only the tinsel is beat up among christmas light rainbows, and the jueras used to come and go as men in North Beach, across from the Fab Mab, got in face inside.

what a tourist crowd likes is illusionists to feed the beast on their dreams. this is for the locals.

"mamacita linda hermosa y preciosa como 'sta la cosa," say slicked back homemade tat men boyfriends out front, between Pancho Villa carne asada tacos for a buck 99 and the liquor store, working/not working macho, effortless tough, don't care. they can be with anyone and what will you say? just "'scuze me," as you slide by, try not to bother a guy smoking and waiting for his woman to finish her number so he can take her down Rondel Place and dead ends, huffing as they go, poor man's rush, and sharpie their names on the wall while fucking.

maybe you don't feel at home anywhere but the Chatterbox, now ironically called Amnesia, where you're the only queer at the punk show holding a pint of Red Tail Ale if you're flush. the picture of Keith Richards gazes down at you, the only art on black walls, from the sound booth, and local bands named after muni lines wreck your ears and you scheme on straight girls because you don't know about femmes. all the same. six pints, and all you're good for is cuddles.

one day you find a room fulla dyke punks and they say, you can mosh if you wanna and you don't have to be drunk. one day you make a band of gay pranksters. one day they open a bar called the Lex. one day all the bois become men and all the femmes stay and love them.

then word gets out every ten years, and the dot communist booms and the techies from Dallas and everyone swarms and says, 'how delicious this culture, let's kill it,' and you spray paint her name in the bathroom and on sidewalks and get into city hall politics and charm them with lusty skills and messenger tricks. you been around. you know how this goes, how to get them to open their wallets.

you make bands in the bars and blend in among muggles and wave magic wands and find out where the hell is Good Vibes anyways this decade. no use crying over $300 apartments once shared with pin cushions and shaved skull revolutionaries. you got worlds to change and venues to open and those lower down in gutters to lift up with your muscle cuz you're grown now and no one can stop you.

this is your town.

she might be crushed and old under the weight of so many men served, so many sick healed, with her heart of gold whores, dykes, fags, trans, beggars, since barbary saloon girls delivered in ships and covered wagons clawed their way to thrones to be queen, but she never sold out.

so you go to her, your whole life, the one you told secrets, how to blow you just right. she carried you through the hardest nights, you pay just to stay up and drink, talk and cry, watch the sun come up and not even use her that way. like an old couple.

you actually give a fuck, but you won't let her give you one though it's her job to love you no matter what, you agree, she'll take all your money at the end. to keep each other alive.

RIP George Michael

we knew you were gay with *Father Figure*. i mean what else could you be?

still, for a long time, only rumors. an ex who dated Seal said she saw you make eyes at him across the pool or was it the pool table at his fancy mansion?

still, you had to be caught in a park bathroom with a cop to come out.

still, nothing changes, even/especially for pop stars, but that was the last sneaky BJ for you.

next a video in mirrored aviators about public sex and shaming us made all ten of us proud as we watched in a san diego gay bar.

still, you got free. now i guess your family will euphemize your death from "complications from pneumonia" or whatever code they're giving it these days. your family consists of straight girls who wanked off to you at 13 because they couldn't see your real family was us.

still the plague makes of us diseased pariahs, even the rich famous successful handsome perfect out ones, even if we were never sick. we stand for the sick. we stand up to those who want to defend your honor by saying you weren't and what? we're better than our dead friends cuz we didn't die of the plague?

you would have tossed that bullshit aside. you stood for us. for you. wear a gold star when you're not jewish. say you're positive when you're negative. you'd do it. although you can't chime in now, i have to believe you would have.

see, i do need another hero. i do have faith. switch a star on your belly. turn systems of privilege and flags upside down. right now truth is monumental, but a lie to make a point is fine, as you always were.

we're sick, and proud of it.

Bowie's Grave

yes, children! recite your lessons. speak out, tear down heroes, shame everyone, spit on graves. die easy knowing one day you'll bless smashings of your image, any homage. cycle destruction, rend society, remote control zombies dumbly stumbling. you understand now. stomp the buddha. Bowie demanded, escape the proscribed.

no gold stars for coloring in lines. not clean or upright. love James Brown and Jerry Lee Lewis. break everything and sleep in what's left. silence = death. looting equals life. choose your store wisely. long loving looks at ugly. shame is compelling. iconoclasm is welcome. to be saints, leaders, and heroes, eschew halos, crowns, and laurels.

dethroned, rockstars saw you through changes and never wanted sainthood, willing to break, sang "break it all."

remake it in your image, as it will be remade again, as your grave will be spat on when you're gone. let loogies water daisies where we fall.

Prince

it was '82, me and my girl we did it one time, said i love you, moved in together. that's how you did.

never considered people might think an interracial couple was something. we were in that love bubble, and it was Oakland. full of black people and white people. no big.

'83 we moved to another hood in Oaktown, an apartment building. still stood out as the black and white dykes. still didn't care.

driving her pickup truck one day, i heard this pornografalsetto song and thought, whoa, who's this chick getting so personal on the radio. then the DJ said, "that was Prince, singing 'Do Me Baby'," and i said, oh shit, i need to pay more attention to this genderfucker.

we moved to the white neighborhood. still standing out. still not caring, but i think it started to wear on us a little, specially her. being the only white dyke in a black hood was different than being the only black dyke in a white neighborhood.

'84, my best friend from hi skool told me he was positive. i got off the phone and broke down.

i sat in the living room that year under the *Gone with the Wind* spoof poster of Thatcher and Reagan with the mushroom cloud in the background.

watched *Mad Max*, *Brother From Another Planet*, *Liquid Sky*, *The Hunger*, *Christiane F*, and *Sid and Nancy*, six times each before returning them to the video store.

drank a million Buds and Slip n Slid with our pals in our wifebeaters and mirrored cop shades before they became wife pleasers. we most definitely were wife beaters beating the hell out of each other over a freebase pipe.

sat in front of grandma's converted TV console, high lacquer cherrywood cabinet full of records and a turntable. drank myself silly to Howlin' Wolf and Lightnin' Hopkins, and Gil Scott and Suzie Quatro and the B-52s.

for hours, listening to Prince's *Controversy*, turning the album cover over in my hands, analyzing. did he really mean it? did he love us that much? was he really saying this?

Am I black or white, am I straight or gay?
People call me rude, I wish we all were nude
I wish there was no black and white,
I wish there were no rules...

we were all alone in a world where christians wanted us dead, but there was Prince, coke and whisky and Starfish and Coffee and Let's Go Crazy and Jack U Off and Annie Christian and *Purple Rain*, a cult crossover hit, and *Under the Cherry Moon*, panned by critics, but he could do no wrong, and ruffled shirts and romance and femme dykes onstage, his spittin image girl versions of him, a narcissist dream of straight-acting queers fucking the mirror like there might be something going on, just like us and our pals, brown and black and white, fags n dykes passing joints at the disco, sexy even if there was a plague, one big cuddle party.

it didn't feel lonesome. it felt right and like motherfuckers better make room for us because if they didn't, we were coming through anyway, led by the most fearless, least fucks-giving motherfucker on the planet with all the moves and a voice that could go from girl to boy in a second. if he wasn't intimidated, neither were we.

'89, me and my records got tossed on the street cuz i got high and everyone was mad.

2016, i'm ashamed now more than i was that day, because when i look to pay homage to the man, i gotta go on the internet like some kinda poser cuz i never bought new Prince records.

the night after he leaves us, it's a full moon, i put on When Doves Cry but it keeps stopping in the middle because everyone in the world is playing it because somewhere along the line we all lost our records.

the clouds are all over the moon. she's real big behind that cloud cover, i can tell. i light the candles and say, come out, you gotta call him home and the clouds part, and i say, i'm sorry, Prince. i lost the records. i'm sorry. it's not that i ever stopped loving you.

i just thought you'd always be there.

Jailbreak Baby Come On

just wait and see they said.
so when they zig, we zag.

see who has to be held close before it's too late.
see what weapons we stashed. escape routes. systems.

see what places are free right now. the Yukon. Berlin. New Zealand.
geographics were never an option.

you gotta get outta the splatter zone to live long enough to save as
many as you can.

you gotta dream of beloveds. call everyone. face cops down on
frozen North Dakota plains under water cannons.

you gotta call to arms. call to poets. call to all the bodies you ever
loved.

meet with fence-sitters and old friends and exes. say, this is who
we are. stand for us.

the polite ones, the rule followers, the make-no-waves people,
they were never with you. they'll smile as they turn away and fill
out their government forms and turn you in and say nothing as
you're carted away.

so give up on smilers. go toward risk takers. rebels.
proclaimers of i will die 4 u.

Things Aretha Taught Me

translate your spiritual life to the secular world so everyone can get closer to humanity.

be a conduit, get impediments out of the way. let something bigger than you flow through you.

be confident in your ability to do just this. the personal is political; your struggles can be made universal. give voice to the lonesome and beat down. shore up those who fight for justice, with song or whatever your service is, and bail money. feel it all, so the stuck can touch even just the basics: mad sad glad.

be a rousing cry as they drive down the road, windows open, yelling. over the years it helps.

have faith, be carried. but don't talk about it unless asked. put the good times out to the world, and bring your deepest heart to the few who invite you in. don't mope. if you're blessed to be surrounded by friends when you're dying, crack jokes. give them the solace you desire.

try a little tenderness.

Dysfunction

enter Donald Trump, exit Leonard Cohen.

wherein Leonard is the teenage boy with *Dog Day Afternoon*
looks, Dick Tater is drunk stepdad, and the whole brood is lifted
up, a rapture of cool. your face is a mess.

Dad? i'm not calling you Dad. cleaning your shotgun, fifth of
rotgut in your crotch. let's wait and see.... till you lose a son and
we're wrecked.

oh, Leonard. what a poet. left us right when this asshole is about
to provide material.

what a sassy boy. sad serious boy. what a big brother who got all
the babes, all the backup singers in his band to jump in his bed
and then become stars. or was it them that made him big?

Leonard's rolling around the record player while Bad Dad rages
over steak and whiskey and how he can grab pussy cuz he's a star.
Leonard stood still till cats came to him.

Leonard! been called asshole himself. knew one when he saw
one. saw trouble and said, "oh, i just realized i had a date at a dive
where a show will replenish the millions my manager stole."

his motives have been questioned. when other guys used lines for
love, he was accused of using love for lines. what kinda guy rats
out Janis for blowing him at the Chelsea, singing about how she
preferred handsome men, but for him she'd make an exception?

what kinda guy beats his knuckles bloody and leaves right when
the biggest loser barges in?

Cohen: "aw fuck this, i gotta go. i'm a lone wolf taking no shit, no family ties. well, there's one, not to this family tho, hope you don't mind, my girlfriend's coming over to tie me to the kitchen chair and cut my hair. hallelujah."

all the other children, we wanna leave early. not everyone is done with their shift though. not everyone has done all their chores though. listened to Dad rant.

not all songs have been sung, instruction manuals of how to commit patricide set on the shelf, color coordinated like the truly literate do. not all movies glorifying the Menendez brothers have been kerchunked into the VCR in the background, blaring.

blink twice if you need us, Melania. never mind, you're getting your due. well, not even Slovenian supermodel First Babe deserves that. everyone's favorite MILF.

we could all bow out the back door. feed the dog under the table, smoke on the porch while Mom does the dishes after cooking the dinner and Dad says, "you know, she works so hard."

"well thank you honey," she calls out from a tub of suds, "thank you for that." he ashes on a dirty plate and burps.

gross. Not My Real Dad. fuck you. you're at the top of my resentment list. we have to process. but i can't even look at you.

we have to talk. but i make it a point not to talk with those who take shots when it's slop and act like they called it.

i may be a shark but i don't take advantage. i've been that guy too drunk to sink it but i have broken a pool cue over a rapist. i'll put an eight-ball in my fist and roundhouse a racist. just waiting for my moment. for you to pass out, a beer dangling from your fingers.

i hitchhiked world tours sewing a red maple leaf on my backpack before you repaired your good standing. till that great new boyfriend moved in, grandpa never liked him, he was so hot. 8 years a grownup running the house. so nice. hot meal every night, no one passed out on the couch, the electricity on when we got home. so proud of us as a family. that guy was Real Dad.

remember when friends escaped to our place because we looked like heroes compared to that frat house with the red black and white flag down the strasse?

and now that mob's chanting HEIL, you on the veranda calling gangs to run out neighbors for genders, colors, or headscarves.

point fingers. it's not you, it's them. no it's you. it's me. we gotta talk but i just can't. can we text?

you say, "have freedom. i trust you. you do not have to spend summer sweltering in the upstairs bedroom i changed my mind, you are not grounded." Yeah, Dick? well, neither are you.

you say, "no really, you deserve everything. a convertible Mustang. a dog. unless you're Indian. or Black or Muslim."

oh, you say, you musta misspoke: the pursuit of happiness is not for everybody. can't they take a joke.

"just lie. whitewash. here, have money, a life. be loved, unless you're queer. have school, for some debt. liquor, speed. take my advice, i'm not using it, just don't be brown. not Arab or Mexican i'll call ICE." but you can't make Indians leave, just fuck up our natural life.

let's forgive Leonard for *Beautiful Losers* because it was just like the title said.

Bad Dad says, "not everyone gets to leave yet because WAIT. you ARE grounded! and your friends have to leave. party's over!"

grounded in race, up to our neck in 'phobes and photos of your boys, sure of themselves after hanging a man, crowded around for a shot, banal as a picnic. someone has to stay and clean up.

Leonard sings to the dead of 2016—Prince, Bowie, Vanity—making us dance, sing and fuck while thinking.

Harper Lee, killing mockingbirds.
Afeni Shakur, 2Pac's Panther mom.
Ali, floating butterfly-like for the revolution.
Elie Wiesel, hunting you.
Gene Wilder, Pryor's straight white man.
Alexis Arquette, who was trans, then gender suspicious.
John Glenn's one small step for man.
Zsa Zsa, who married 9 men (a refugee from Hungary's gotta keep herself in jewelry), most famous for slapping a cop.
Princess Leia, facing down evil empires.
and her mom, who wouldn't stay without baby.

party now, broken home runaways.
Leonard can pay for everything he broke.

Nancy Reagan and Phyllis Schlafly can hold up the wall, just say no, fall on deaf ears, no to power, rights, Black America, curing AIDS, Ladies Against Women. women against gays, wrapped in cellophane, greet your man at the gate with a pitcher of martinis, and feminism will just go away.

Leonard smoothly assuages, swaying, raises his arm to catch the bride's bouquet. ah, the beautiful dead. maybe Janis is up for more head.

we'll hold it down, dragging egos tied to our bumpers all the way to Standing Rock. won't take a badge, posing with bikers just to say we went somewhere. we'll see what's needed, or if we're more of a suck on resources than a blow to the man.

Leonard and Prince, prepare us the way.

storm security, jump onstage yell in the mic, instruments of peace. in the pit, aggression release.

Not My Real Dad, don't tell me what to do with your skinhead pals in that backyard party. not alt as in different, alt as in old skool, good old fashioned third reich, around the keg, breaking kneecaps of punk icon cool kids who visit from down the road. they heard about us. Biafra still limps.

watch where you slam, headbanger, throwing elbows in girls' eyes, hands in panties of those who surf crowds. cuz everyone knows, The Punks Are All White.

Leonard left us in charge, power of the mic, swinging on a long cord whipping over heads, slung with a deft hand. knock you out, knock em dead, reel it back keep singing, not missing beats, call you out. rile up the crowd.

might be you, trampled this time, unnoticed, passed out, under souls of oxblood docs.

thank you! and good night.
no we don't have an encore.
and we're not cleaning up the blood this time.

New Year's Eve at the Sleater-Kinney Concert

demarcations of new years, new angles on old fights, new love for girls you have known for years and looked away, now in your hands, fingers around her hips like the double barrel handles of an automatic at the arcade, point and shoot, bad guys falling, rock stars calling you to choose your weapon. boy brings another bass, tuned, primed, loaded to empty on the crowd.

meat men's job: not removing girls but balloons from between barriers and rock god movie moguls in houndstooth business-lady suits who say, "laugh's on you, big guy," mimicking Angus Young in a kilt, "call me a middle-aged white girl, true, it was a problem with the movement, working on it, but look! i still run your world," she telepaths direct to the new Old Boy Network boy, thirty-year-old yawning, hoping to be noticed by queen of the swarm—sorry, she's taken—looking to get laid by riots in the body of a girl to which he wanked, born addicted and ejected from a northwestern teen hormone womb of heroin and heroines.

no one told the Bouncer it now means girls can bounce balls in the air, triumphant, to the songs of two dead men fucking with gender roles, Michael n Bowie, shouting from the stage, floor, hallowed halls of rock in frocks, anthems of queer children, confessions of outcasts and cyphers, secret rebel torn dress messy-faced malformations of generations who hid in books and manifested invisibility only to later parade their way across the boards and wake up others who pretend to be bored but are really just numb because nerves have been yanked from them, plucked, strangled, pounded like the crazy piano player who raised the hood and put objects on wires to recreate sounds of pain and fire and, hitting ivories, made nightmares for grownups, made them pay for dissonance and pretend to like it.

these children for whom dissonance is still all that makes sense, grow like vines around old trees, and, still green, face the sun, light shining through them.

at midnight she turns to you, and through the sugar and caf special recipe famously unknown the world over to be the taste of capitalism, the bottle drained and dropped by gods who must be crazy, great served ice cold in snow, enjoyed by Santa in the North Pole, even you can see this moment will be the through line of the rest of your years, the suspension piano wire on which you will zip over jungles, macho machete dangling from fingers topping trees just enough to get an aromatic mix, throw it in an abalone shell and light it with a torch, as you, slung low in your sliding swing, swoop over baobabs, lopping off just enough verdure to let light in, rival macaws and reveal monkeys who raise a banana in salute to the gods of our time, and girls, who, riding on the shoulders of men, spur you on and see space as just another desert to cross to find a star to land on, to raise cats and pit bulls and make the music of the spheres to ring out in snow globes, a shield or a dome for sound waves to ricochet and settle us all into dreams with a note that holds, everlasting.

Forty-Five

i got your 45 hanging eyes like 45s
broken record going round
everyone's high on fentanyl
you got to ask yourself
why would dealers spike a piece of their pie?

same reason robber barons want you to die
dare you to breathe white lines derived
from mystery sources
you think ups but you're going down
same slide that killed your friends

favorite game is put the fear of gods in you
and grease all over your shades
so you can't see what's happening
to the gritty life you made in this city
layers of historical union with all that is
through the ingestion of plants that enable vision
a minefield.

you shouldn't have to risk your life for a little blow,
said the hag who somehow survived the '90s
despite her best efforts
who once hid scabs under a hawk hanging in her eyes
floppy enough to fuck up facial recognition
surveillance cameras on every corner

gotta do what you gotta do to survive life
sometimes involves crack coke meth dope
and you shouldn't die trying to live
murder by death said Lemmy
loved him some dykes backstage passing mirrors

he always got the pure stuff
in days when Hells Angels guaranteed their shit
and delivered it to their living god
who played for bikers in stretch jeans
cowboy boots mutton chops
and a mole to scare a jackal posing as your granny

bass leveled at your head
and a whole trailer hitched to a tour bus
loaded with Jack Daniels and crank
but for lowly little old you

it's just to drown out a bad childhood
swerve around mental cement posts
next thing you know you're levitating over your body
deciding to stay or go
by then it seems a good time to leave
no pain no pain
once outside the physical realm
you realize you're free.

and don't that make land grabbers happy.
no one needing services and crying
losing minds
tagging your names in your own yellow shit on sidewalks
because if you're not gonna be famous at least be known
be a menace
an annoyance to those schooled in Pacific Heights
private ivy leagues Specific Whites

free to set up million dollar baby condos
like neutron bombs.
kill people
save buildings
kill crops

grow HIV
life is cheap

get the gold
or just a clean sidewalk to a latte at a cafe cooled
by fog rolling in the gate
no human wrecks to step over who stayed out late
overdosing in the summer of your
vile lives.

i got their 45 hanging
eyes like 45s
broken record going round and round
i got a 45
i bought on the corner.
they're going down.

II.
A Call to Arms

Poet Found Wandering on Material Plane

i may be broke and get pulled over for not doing paperwork i thought i did but didn't, but i was in the army, so i bottom good to uniforms.

i'm in love with a babe who thinks my words are magic so it's fine, even though i drive away from the police after blinding them with fairy dust feeling uncomfortably warm. what is that, shame? so ubiquitous i never named it.

–dear god please don't let her see how much i fuck up.
–she already said she saw it all and she loves you anyway so calm down.
–ok

i can't figure out how to keep my pants up and disguise my body as a boy's at the same time which probably isn't working cuz i have a girl's ass probably but who knows since i never look at it.

i discover suspenders but go through em quick they snap off and flip over your head and whack you in the nose it's clownish.

who knew if you wear em you better know how to fix em but i'm missing the fixit brain cell. the femme is a mechanical mind. because what it takes to fix things is patience.

i could be a patient but they can never catch me long enough to tie me to a bed. speaking of beds i tied the mosquito net to the finial on the lamp over hers to repair the princess fort.

fingers crossed.

Glamour

that fake brokeback coat ain't warm.
that road better be salt.
this child's hardscrabble.
this child got pride.

makes monuments out of mud buckets.
lifts up the poor on a ski lift.
a man with money thinks he can turn her. he's a snowball and
she's the eternal flame of the tomb of the unknown soldier.

she smiles at a man when she says, "nope," pretty enough to look
like, "oh yes baby," like the glare on his windshield driving him off
the road, like long hair covering naked, on a cliff driving sailors
to rocks.

we go skipping off over alpine meadows to sleep with baby sheep.
death is only tragic if you care.
and how could you care for a machine dressed like a prince?
everyone has a glamour.

hers is pretty things, and harmless child, and so is theirs.
theirs is love, and protection, and i'll take care of you,
i'll do what you say, here's my heart.
hers is small and human and tender,

but underneath that worn blanket, little match girl shivering, is
a colossal, under that child working cuteness you'd never know
was a girl strung out on the promise of a capitalist dream, hopeful
little dyke on a shoestring budget, in a scatter of stars,

through a time tunnel to a palace on the edge of a galaxy guarded
by gods that smite a motherfucker with one back hand.

they got no idea.
they just see a babe with a smile in her eyes.

In the Land of the Seers

the man on the street rhapsodizes: "oh, 1992, that was a year, money everywhere." city shamans tell us what's really happening, dodging institutions, dodging Haldol raining down like bullets from the sky on Fourth of July.

they run from the ordered life. revel in the summertime. the sewers have something to say, loud singing into the summer morning, "we are here, evidence, leavings of trekkers climbing to the timberline through the Tenderloin, cooler than bear scat with its berries and bells and smelling like mace, cool like Ella, but more authentic, clues of entrails of those with nowhere to go."

the High Priestess tunes in to prophecies wafting on air like sound. she stops before ducking in to anoint the feet of holy whores in front of the Ambassador Hotel, sanctuary for the forsaken, last stop of the sick, monastery of St. Hank, where some five memorials a day once transpired in his office in the time of the plague, where residents would say a few words like "he was a sonofabitch but he was my friend and friends are hard to come by."

silently she says to the channeler, ah, yes, '92, that was a year. i was guided. i was 7. i saw the earth break like waves in an orchard in the great quake of '89 in Watsonville. i learned, fear nothing. now where is that fabled money and where should it fall like ripe fruit?

they touch as they pass. between them a dazzling globe of electric fire, blue lightning, hovers and explodes with a loud report, as Crowley said, knocking out a cop as he hands a jaywalking ticket to a man with no reason to believe in crosswalks, leaving behind the fresh clean smell of ozone.

Shiner

to fight by your side, the privilege, the pleasure is mine.
to paraphrase a mighty goth fag, all the greats in stark black and
white or technicolor boost.

the power of a butch in priests robes (sing hallelujah), the power
of Baldwin running it down to Cavett, the power of a gun in the
hand of a woman, the power of a mic in the hand of a femme, the
power of your hand on the flat of my chest, the power of a bike
ride in biblical downpours and waterproof socks to succor you
through war.

so much vaseline on the lens. you are the shiner of spectacles, of
a fist to my face in a frenzy of light from a tower to ships among
rocks. may you always.

Meditation

you rummage through panty drawers, find something to cover heaven. i stare.

whatever one meditates on, accessed throughout the day. stress. calvins. paradise.

naked is the first word. i pull you close before you charge around the world. follow like a puppy.

as you point out, you're usually right. captain my captain.

i call the shots at night when you have no defenses, your heels off the cliff, my two fingers on your chest pushing you ever so.

you fall slow mo, as i have for years, imperceptible. don't care about nets. they only stop us from destinies.

all death is little.

The Beloved and the Bestie

the beloved has a friend date with the artist, the feminist, the fervent and laser-sharp beautiful androgen, the two of them a force, walking streets of Paris, Florence, or the Mission.

tonight they convene a two queer G20, planning world domination, smoking and drinking in a yard that won't take whacking but keeps overgrowing irrepressible blooms disguised as weeds.

whenever she teams up, it's with the handsomest and purest of heart, the descendants of soldier poets reliving heroism around fires, remembering lines by alliteration.

each child over the age of three sports a scar where the truth became known and naiveté was unceremoniously dumped by the side of the road in that pull-over, back-door-open, roll-the-body-out-and-scatter-gravel way.

she loves those with a veneer that blinds would-be invaders to their one flaw, gaping maw of divine influence, sacred revelation, that hides the spot in a shadow where you lean over a railing into the roiling sea. the irresistible outside makes the viewer, no matter how hateful, love the view.

when the trance is lifted, all that's left is space, nowhere to attach ire. or maybe it's dark matter invisibly holding whole galaxies in place. "you go get that old punk," says the witch, momma healer old soul encased in soft youth, sailing out wisdom in the voice of a child.

there's value in old punks? maybe a Ramone or an Iggy. no idea what he looks like. he needs help dressing himself. confused by his body. by age. looks in the mirror and sees a stranger. his grandmother and great-grandfather. Indians and priests. looks at her and the spell's broken. of the illusion of self and alienation.

he looks up at the troposphere. it always has ideas. "see? can't tell by looking. sunny blue sky, in it a million invisible stars. most beautiful girl in the world, and yet she loves you."

The Call

the beloved is quiet in the aftermath of her friend's rape, who doesn't want to call it that because if you call it that, you have to deal with everything that means.

she honors and listens and calls me to honor and listen, to hear what happened to everyone, to how we have to frame experience to preserve dignity.

i have held it up to my mother's light, to her darkness, to a knife and a threat and a gang of russians wreaking vengeance she watched out a window, but it was like it happened to her, of american soldiers hired to save, but all conquerors take what they want.

and retelling to cops who ask for every detail. it would seem one does have control over that. so why did you relive it?

the beloved's voice is muted. her words parsed. she knows every time she offers her services to hear confessions of the assaulted she must acknowledge in silence her crucifixions, bear the suppliant's burden and go to the next, touch on the story that has already been told, who then nods and says yes, aloud, i as well, it's still here, brutality we can't understand that we come back to contemplate or fight. it makes no sense to lie down in the arms of attackers.

maybe we die standing, refusing, asking why. maybe we take up arms, an army of lovers. maybe we believe all time happens at once, bodies, passivity, action. maybe we're buccaneers. maybe in this moment we forget that we have cut off ears.

justice served. personally in the privacy of his home. slavers executed in their sleep. a thousand miles walked at night. snakes slept with. secrets murmured. we refuse to die, live, submit, shut up, dress or act according to the whimsical systems of others. at once peasants and heads of state, we slash through underbrush to get to our insides. discover how to hold it. we buttress each other. put our shoulders into it. we study the past and know everything.

we come back to earth to know what only sensation can tell, to find in the body more than is ever divulged in the starry womb of god.

The Revolution Inside

–i hate them, she says.
–me, too, he says.

he's a man-hating man. no platitude or gratitude will solve it
tonight. no amount of what's good about how far we have come.
she'd still have to deal with it, even if overall, if cops didn't wield
power, if dudes weren't less dickly than a thousand years ago.

he wishes he were helpful. offers to come over but she cherishes
this night alone in her palace, where she's sovereign and needs no
man. no protection. no fixing.

all he can say is, yeah that happened to me. i rifled through what
i coulda done to prevent it. even blaming myself is a measure of
control. that's how we do. he doesn't want her to ever feel that
way, but it means she's there for everyone it happens to, because
it's happened to everyone.

they'll never second guess themselves. they know the enemy.
they take the badassery of witches queers and harlots throughout
history to the grave.

there are two ways to love a girl. one is pretend to be perfect and insist on being right, even when she can see you're wrong. the other is let her see yourself, and hope for the best.

there's a night bird outside the window, singing, "with a love like that, you know you should be glad." the Beatles were good once. they had their day. Yoko found John for a minute before it all went to shit. i'm sure they don't regret the glass house where they lived, looking over the Hudson straight into Hoboken.

they were the couple i could hold up to the light when my own parents were too grounded in reality to sit in bed for a week in all-white sheets and protest the Viet Nam war. they thought commies needed to be stopped, since Mom ducked under the iron curtain by the skin of her ass, and everyone liked Ike.

John and Yoko were having more fun than my parents. my dad had a mustache when other dads were shaved smooth. my dad voted for Kennedy, who got shot before we could draw a clear bead on where he stood with Nam. he got out of the life before he could be blamed. he was leaning away from it. that's what got him bumped off, said Mom, too dovish. him and Jackie looked like they were having fun in Cape Cod. him and Monroe looked like they were having fun in underground tunnels between cabins at casinos till Lawford came along.

Hanoi Jane looked like she was having a good time with the Viet Cong. Cassius Clay dropped his slave name, went by Ali and refused to kill. my parents looked askance at heroic rebel maneuvers. he had his own backyard war. the Panthers were at it in Oakland, enough fire power to shut down the OPD. "just trying to serve some lunch, officer. don't shoot."

all the working class parents, single moms, mechanics and plumbers whose wives picked up popular kids in Cadillacs, they saw straight through it. don't blame them, they voted for McGovern.

this girl and me, we will love in white beds and city apartments and lie down for peace and write songs and wear flowers in our hair. because really what else is there?

the beloved with her time away builds castles in the air and on the ground and on the swelling sea, standing on her clam shell raft without so much as a barge pole, the way she turns, she covers all the parts of her she doesn't want anyone to see.

she thinks, clears her mind, says a thing and manifests it. closes her eyes, draws to her philanthropists descended from a long line of hipster-headed angels, the one uncorrupted billionaire that hasn't quite rotted from the inside yet because it's hard not to have spots all over you, like Kaposi, like flesh-eating bacteria. when you are made of money, you just start collapsing in on yourself, but right before you die, you seize injustice by the horns and wrestle it to the ground, because you see in that moment that you are no different than a junkie queer madman ranting on the street.

the beloved magnetizes saints before they vaporize, pulls them to her. super-heroes find themselves in a sugar shack puppy pile gazing up at her, silhouetted, gigantic against the Spank Me to Heaven billboard. it's rhetorical. it's ironic. it will be her dishing out punishments, corporal or otherwise.

she receives adjurations, appeals, solemn solicitations. holy, she instructs. the oracle incarnate, over the fissure in the earth where the mystic vapor of hallucinogenic steam rises, and she gazes into the bowl of Kassotis spring water in one hand, laurel branch in the other, its leaves whispering to her.

in a purple cloak over a small white toga, she takes the sacrifice, baby goat set upon the altar. if it trembles, it's a good day for prophecy. it shivers, and she watches the fear of the world. she bathes in holy water. she sprinkles the floor with holy water. she reads the future to her supplicants. Alexandrian librarians smuggle her hexameters, as Christians raze the stacks, as Spartans die like she said, their iron coins weighing their pockets. they bring gold back from the wars and are conquered. love of money and nothing else will ruin Sparta, she counsels the mighty.

Ministry

she wades in the water, moves houses with bare hands, brings
bottomless baskets of bread. when the people ask, they receive.

apprentice. do as she says, hand out the things, field requests,
listen to stories. won't go in the water with your blue suede laces.

she's bolder than you, no fucks, they have to be earned over years,
deed by deed, earnest speeches when you think you're no good at

16th Street venues but you'll think of something once that mic's
in your hand and women stand before you.

she snapped polaroids of you, like you did of her, at every turn.
filed them away. snapshots of when you gave a speech in the cold

or carried a sign at 6am or handed socks into hobbit houses
through doors cracked, to voices that answered yes, i need.

what she values.
what is valid.

you never saw it as something you could do, never listened to
Harvey, or Harry, or Cleve until the veil was flipped.

get out of your vaudeville act and do what you came here to do.
electrify. a track star looking to ride a meteor's tail.

the saint glides through her swing moves so easy, an inside job,
not a master class. starts with a heartbeat for all creatures.

she says: everyone wants to, has godhood inside.
all you have to do is show them. watch and learn.

your leading has been in insignificant realms. wake and pray
for a minimum of mayhem, to learn with a whisper not a brick,

a bloodless rebellion, a cuban missile crisis,
where we see what might have been and avert it,

stack the cans, dig the bunkers, skip to peace and butterflies
that seem dead then fly away, just napping.

prove medieval ravers wrong with their false premonitions
because they ate the wrong mushroom

because they burned their grandmothers at the stake
because they wanted power but forgot to save wisdom

because they never cared about light so threw their clouded vision
over us, a thousand-year wet blanket, folded and moldy,

and told us it was destiny.
find other truffles and begin again.

Shooting Stars

the girl goes shooting and shopping for a blade she'll name after a
witch who famously spun onstage for queers coming of age.

braves flash floods and thunderstorms to fire off rounds with
sister barrio queens who push out what occupies and destroys,

to regenerate in wide open acreage.
they build mansions, don't they?

whoever promises warm lairs, leaves out the part about how small
it is inside. she's spent her life in target practice, armories stocked,

heart stoked, walls sledge hammered quick as underworld 3D
printers can build them. she makes gifts of protection, which is

the same as magic. finds crystals everywhere. they arrive in boxes
from long lost uncles, noteless.

guided to secret campsites by signs carved in trees, she finds clear
stones coming out of the ground like a glass spring. fast learner,

she started in utero with tomes on caring, books on ceremony,
took them in osmotically, still listens when i read, saying,

this sounds familiar. we don't pass knowledge to each other on
the main road. too public. we write it on paper and leave it on

tops of rehearsal space bathroom door frames to be found and
smoothed out like a treasure map, interactive,

with different paths to riches. list what you will not do, he writes.
receives a blank paper and keeps it in his wallet.

climb swim or fly, but get me. let me bring a screwdriver on a tool
belt, jimmy the lock as she sits suspended from a rope around

hips, a swing. swinging hips, how she mesmerized enemies.
i leave charms at her place. consider retrieval. pull over at treasure

island, last chance for u-turns before tower of power's home town.
meditate on a tyrant skyline. she's defiant in the eye of hurricanes,

daring disasters to disrupt. i'll leave them talismans to soak in her
dreams, hallowed by Custer-killers, raptors on telephone poles,

devouring songbirds, fucking in freefall, mating for life,
diplomats, race traitors, killers of each other's fathers, sell outs,

indian school dropouts, working for peace. they can't stand still.
gotta move, gotta fix wrongs. choose the next leader of gangs to

gallop down hills. they see it now. whitey said he'd take the land.
his word was good. they search airwaves,

find us, desperate.
fill us with roses and lightening.

she rides, skates, surfs. i let her stare.
nothing to lose but cool.

And what is cool, but a handful of
glass beads traded by wolves for a continent?

Portugal, post-Salazar

i. Lisboa

stones in the sidewalk are slippery in the rain like soapstone so everyone gets to walk in the narrow street.

there is hardly any hate except the same old hate: there has to be an outlet, a recipient, a scapegoat like the trans woman who was beaten by children raised in a shelter who had their own issues of abandonment and self hate. they had to. they had to turn it on her, on someone, didn't they?

everywhere misogyny echoes, give up the scepter or take it on. we pay and pay.

ii. Fado

in the cafes the people sing *fado*, Portuguese folk music like mafioso singing opera in convertibles in black and white movies with Marcello and Sophia, they had it when they had nothing else, when fascism ruled. they clung to it. they were told to by Salazar, as if they needed him to instruct them: *fado futbol fatima*.

fado, smooth drive you can't resist when they sing to you low like fucking you, they come up and flirt like marlene in a white tux. they touch your shoulder, men singing to bald men of long curly locks, femmes come up behind butches with a hand on the shoulder. a game like soccer, a fervor like the virgin envisioned by children as pure and as reverently played.

anarchy comes in the cafe and sings a song for free. american hustler asks for a fistful of dollars? no escudo, no silver exchanged, just a slice of chorizo in the low light and fingers dancing on a mandolin or a Parisian ex-pat playing jazz on a bucket and a string.

iii. *The Resistance*

in the midst of intellectuals locked up, communists beaten, queers made to stand for hours and days, questioning and prisons as old as the inquisition and older, churches across from prisons, medieval strongholds that still threaten, never fall, thick stone walls, now a museum, then a place to keep shelves full of notes on your private life, nothing private.

and the mothers who fought, who kept the world in their hearts, who barely had any love left for their children, who left latchkey kids to raise themselves, to find a crust of bread on big oak tables while they murmured, heads bent low over a kerosene lamp making zines on printing presses pushing the curtain aside to keep a lookout for the secret police, the PIDE. why do the secret police need so many letters? it means "be afraid." but the mothers of children who grew up to make films, to be drafted, to pull up their tanks and their automatic weapons in front of the capitol, they were never afraid enough to stop.

having only had time to criticize their children or lay the back of their hands across their faces, small ancient women show up at poetry readings. they stand and receive applause. they smile upon wide-eyed americans staring down the shadow of fascism. they make amends with their daughters. they have time before they die to smile on their Pippi Longstockings who watched their heroic mamas from afar and told stories of them in empty tree houses in the woods.

and so we go to the only restaurant in town that serves at midnight, we ring the bell. the door opens, and upon seeing writers and filmmakers, they let us in and feed us bread and meat and wine

and water in the low light and the leather and green wood, nothing
changed since the '40s, resistance eternal.

we discuss the book from brazil on how jesus is a trans woman
and turn the magnifying glass around.

and then we are wrapped braided sleeping like that, and my hands searching found you, that part, and i lay my fingers over you and the fingers of my other hand curled around your forehead and that was heaven and shall remain heaven for all time at work or war or onstage belting out anthems and playing any of seven harps in key, you fitting perfect all around me in my arms.

beyond polaroids, it's surround sound with the rain pouring down. it knows when we've come and gone, like a mother singing us to slumber and while opening curtains and setting out pinafores and britches, salt pork and porridge. and then we slid this small boat pushing it through a Lisboan alley to a canal, and there was Susie Bright and Honey Lee Cottrell, if Honey Lee had lived not smoked Marlboros in the bath in that famous pose. Honey Lee had propped up her 35mm Nikkormat next to a clawfoot tub of bubbles and caught them laughing like there was no tomorrow, but there was.

tomorrow came, and if this was that tomorrow, none of the romance had gone, not diminished by time or death, in that same position, Honey leaned up against the cool stern of the boat, and Susie up against her. and we with our eyes full of hope and our mouths full of fresh fucked, waited for the boatman to say go, and we pushed off into the Venetian river, past Arabic tile and Egyptian columns and closed each other's eyes just to feel our fingertips on our faces, because we had all the history in the world, and never had to go hungry.

all we needed was each other, and water, and vessels to carry us through.

Toast

to the beloved
to under the cover of night
where the madman is holy
as you my soul are holy
said Ginsberg
to all his boy heroes
to music played
standing side by side
looking out at hordes
flanked by a battalion
of pied pipers.
here is my profession of heart.

Morning Prayers

the beloved reads next to me, after several hours in line for fry bread at the two-spirit powwow, reading 75 pages of the book for book club, of which she is president. she'll always be president of something, and i'm glad these little things she runs, like how to take care of people and how to house people and navigate silly hall, none of it precludes her always getting more naked than me.

she can always improv one more thing, if it's good and by a shallow creek. when she does long favors, she's so high, her kiss like a sip of tea, like a bee sting. anyone who gets her attention never forgets. maybe they had a quick chance and squandered it, boozy and young. an old bastard who's circled the globe appreciates perfection. recognizes. worships.

i put my forehead on the silk wrapped part of her. reach up to her collarbone. kiss her like i might never again or never thought i would. everyday i put down an offering so she'll be noticed, her name in lights, bonfire in a garbage can, note in a boat put out to sea:

through the miracle of fiber optics, she bends light, shines it in my eye, which constricts, to not let in too much, heart dilates, portals open, deluge, i float out, seeing all filtered through a quasar, which is just a black hole that overeats stars and spits them out. daily i pray, everything's crushed to create.

Church Doors

all that is, help this child that is me who holds her slight body in my hands, to send her off with wishes for us, glitter osmosis, armor invisibility, glamour, to shine to who we gotta shine to, who's gotta see us, give us protection, or steer around us, and also not shine to invaders and cops we need to duck out from.

in the shower across the light box, her winged heart in punk manicure hands. i glance up, take too long to look at something not mine. she'll laugh, call me a creep. knows my heart is right, not throwing her down in fists full of lapels.

biker dads and cheerleaders getting free with trapping tools like knives and belts and no no no. no looking no boyfriend no. means yes to play and church doors opening, slow, the only caveat.

in the night wake to find her always up close like a koala. the proof is in the subconscious. in the morning when she stands barefoot looking at clothes, i just want to be that dirty floor so i could be touching her.

just want to listen to her in the next room reverse-parenting the mom who rescues everything within reach. to study her. fit in little spaces.

put stars in her eyes til she cries, says, it's all too much, falling in love with you so fast.

i hear her in the morning planning horseback rides in salt air, focused, mad for life.

Ode to Mykki Blanco
(My Prounouns Are I You We)

Mykki raps wrath to men condescending
how they'll pay him
"this ain't a hobby!"
calls us to him,
"circle up circle up,"
tales from the periphery
a hymn of stolen property.
balls of lightning shoot out his hands
at a history of bastards.

what's the deal with pronouns?
why align with fuckheads?
times like #UsToo why choose this team
of not so righteous dudes?
to be as in a life briefly recalled
as we squoze down the long hall
holy said Ginsberg
are those between worlds.
be exceptions.
straighten the rest out.

Hey you guys, i mean friends
this way to humanity!
model correct behavior,
change other men?
someone's gotta.... prolly Them.
in the OG sense they
were the enemy
as in them Against Me!
Then They became Us
Guided by guts we went

from punks
to old dykes—
1 tran, 2 trans
they! bold leap out of binary bins.
–pronouns? refuse em
–make up some
shake up cis-tems ascribed to parts and
confuse em.

girls are so cool.
sometimes i wish i was one.
men get free tickets to everything
professional sports? tom of finland?
that's hot.

i'm more like a mascot.
hey you guys,
i mean people….
pronoun showdown with
the guy at home depot
he don't know
sir ma'am sir
spotlight on me now.
whole store is staring
–what now Mykki Blanco?
you said, "i'm a gay man,
but my trans journey's who i am."
abandon us fugitives?
no, you stand with us,
let us see into the mutable deep,
free us.

they say explain yourself.
–tired of educating.
i would claim they themselves

if we're gonna go plural
how bout the royal We?
—i was never a king.
what's in your boxers?
none-ya
like Drew from Trap Girl
n Star Amerasu,
we're hawking
truth loogies
into the mouths of babes
like birdies waiting at the foot of stages
—we got drawers fulla rage
—that's what
—now Mykki Blanco,
lead us out.
we're bleeding out.
Jack H covered masculinity.
it's all toxicity.
i wanna be a man like Mykki.
fingers splayed, wrist cocked,
mic stand flung across
shoulders, classic Cooper Lee
galvanizing
tucked/untucked,
won't be androgenized,
fucked, unfucked.

—you instruct us:
we must protect black children.
we must protect black trans women.
eradicate prisons.
still need abolition.
race me, full of grace
embrace maleness
show up for your own ass,

goddess incarnate.
dare us call your manliness toxic.
we're the beloved who loves you,
reason for all moves.
throw us skyward, trust.
–you'll land in the midst of us.

Free Will

you done it for so many reasons: obligation, should, oughta, learned to. to become an expert. keep love alive. reciprocate. calm. the rent. power over, thinly cloaked. couldn't say no. as a thank you, please, lullaby. a test. to prove you're the best.

they deserved it. they always got what they wanted. they wouldn't take no for an answer.

you loved them. they wanted you. you were used to giving up what was wanted, especially if it was you.

to feel. to avoid feeling.

pact. contract. unspoken promise. currency. service. job. career queer. made it your business. hints. clues. you better.

you done it for so many reasons besides falling unbridled, drawn undeniable. magnet. gravity. orbit. mind of its own. down lonesome highways and stay right beside her. songs from the subconscious. headlights. dreams. the actual fuck.

you've always known the only good reasons are to be all ways, naked in caves, on cliffs, in clouds, by small fires, in rain, drinking white lightning from each other. wonder.

Salt Water

he dreams of drowning when he's always been a good swimmer, of the backseat when he's always driving, of a port that makes shooting dope easy when it was always speed and old faithful, of tentacles that reach into impossibly high land where he had felt safe.

doesn't like not being dad. scrambles for footholds. stumbles. she ducks out of the way in her own tempest tossed boat. he grabs the air, glad she's so nimble as to not be pulled down.

she knows they need time in separate dinghies talking to wide cloudless skies with parched lips, nothing but salt sea, plenty of time to rig up a sail horizontally to catch condensation, a few drops to drink.

they'll meet on that island that reappears over the horizon in its illusory vast empty ocean. for now it's just this moment and this and this like he always said forgetting some of these are crises.

but the stars have faith in them even when their faith waivers. they say, your love is strong. wander in deserts and throngs and the motionless sea without waves or wind, so that when you see each other you fall into each other so gratefully and build sanctuaries. love each other as only those who have died can do.

Pit Bull Bath

a certain kind of dog who looks tough and eats everything alive
and dead—screen doors and squirrels—hides fears. only lets the
boy see.

boy branches out from showers, a morning magnesium bath.
calls the certain kind of dog in. cups water for the dog to drink.

says, "up up." dog raises a paw. brings it back. thinks about it.
hangs out. boy talks softly to the dog, "it's ok."

both paws up on the side. the boy gets up.
dog jumps in. boy gets out.

as he pours shampoo, he says, "see? it's ok, boy."
blue beach towel. keeps the dog spray off his naked body.

"it's ok, boy," he says.
"we can try new things."

How to Write a Book and Explain Everything

books write themselves. all you have to do is ride your bike up a hill while talking to the dead. specially today. and say thank you to every friend and grandma who crossed, and every beast that ever died on your watch. that whole litter of kittens, when you never fixed the cats cuz you were high? and they came here with their tabs for ears just long enough to teach you the body is finite, but love isn't, to let go, that you have no control, that sometimes your stay here is short, and as each tiny cat died, you buried them in the backyard, and that one who was coughing, you put next to the heater in the bathroom, and when you looked in the morning he was dead, and you cried so hard. that one. you gotta thank that one and say you're sorry you did it wrong and thanks and you hope he comes back as a butch dyke's dog. then just open the laptop. stare. start typing.

Acknowledgments

thank you Steph Joy for seeing this was a book, Jen Joseph for making it into one, COMMANDO (Juba Kalamka, Honey Mahogany, Drew Arriola-Sands, Andy Meyerson, Travis John Andrews, Van Jackson-Weaver) for putting words to music, and The Homobiles for healing with punk, Aria Sa'id for believing in me and making it rain, Cynthia Vice, Sam White Swan-Perkins, and Abby Abinanti for including me, Wendy Delorme and Alice Azevedo for translating, Raquel Freire, Valerie Mitteaux, Anarchicks, Suwanne Jo, and everyone who ever took a chance and said fine, come here, read a poem, maybe it will change a thing.